PR

THE

A focus on Jesus Christ, the Way,

the Truth, the Life

DAVID KONSTANT

Fount

An Imprint of **HarperCollins***Publishers*

Fount Paperbacks is an Imprint of
HarperCollins*Religious*
Part of HarperCollins*Publishers*
77–85 Fulham Palace Road, London W6 8JB

First published in Great Britain in 1981
by Collins Liturgical Publications as part of
Jesus Christ, The Way, The Truth, The Life.
This edition first published in 1996 by
Fount Paperbacks

1 3 5 7 9 10 8 6 4 2

© 1981, 1996 David Konstant

A catalogue record for this book is
available from the British Library

000 6280064

Nihil obstat: Anton Cowan
Imprimatur: Philip Harvey, Bishop in North London Westminster,
5 January 1981

Printed and bound in Great Britain by
Caledonian International Book Manufacturing Ltd, Glasgow

CONTENTS

ACKNOWLEDGEMENTS

The publishers are grateful for permission to use the following copyright material:

Quotations from the Bible are from *Jerusalem Bible*, © 1966, 1967 and 1968, Darton, Longman & Todd, and Doubleday & Co. Inc.

Psalm texts are from *The Psalms: a new translation*, © 1963 The Grail (England), published by Collins.

Pages 2–88 are an expansion of material that appeared in its original form in *Congress Prayer Book*, © 1980 National Pastoral Congress Committee.

The verses from 'Day is done', 'Where true love' are by James Quinn SJ, from *New Hymns for All Seasons*, © 1969, published by Geoffrey Chapman.

The verses 'Christ be near at either hand' are a translation of St Patrick's Breastplate by J. Fennelly, from *People's Mass Book*, M. H. Gill & Son.

Excerpts from the English translation of the Rite of Baptism for Children copyright 1969, and from the English Translation of the Roman Missal, copyright 1973, International Committee on English in the Liturgy. All rights reserved.

PREFACE

The word 'gospel' means 'good news'. The four Gospels are distinct accounts of this good news. St Mark begins his account: 'The beginning of the good news of Jesus Christ, the Son of God' (Mark 1:1). When the disciples were sent out by Jesus on their apprenticeship mission, Jesus told them: 'As you go, proclaim the good news, "The kingdom of heaven has come near" ' (Matthew 10:7). And when Jesus was in the synagogue at Capernaum at the start of his mission he said, 'The Spirit of the Lord is upon me, because he has anointed me to bring good news to the poor. He has sent me to proclaim release to the captives and recovery of sight to the blind, to let the oppressed go free, to proclaim the year of the Lord's favour' (Luke 4:18–19). For St John, all was summed up in the Word: 'In the beginning was the Word, and the Word was with God, and the Word was God … and the Word became flesh and lived among us, and we have seen his glory, the glory as of a father's only son, full of grace and truth' (John 1:1,14).

The Word himself was the Good News. Jesus was the Word and the words he spoke were God's words; he gave expression to God. His whole life was in every sense godly. Those who saw him – and really knew him – saw and knew the true glory of God, full of grace and truth. He brought good news to others and showed them how close God was to them. He did this by what he said and did. He freed them from all kinds of slaveries, helped them discover a fullness of life, healed them, forgave them, gave them strength.

The evangelists put into their own words what Jesus said and did, so that others could grasp the good news and make it their own. As St John put it: 'He came as a witness to testify to the light, so that all might believe through him' (John 1:7). These four Gospels are only a beginning for us. They enable us to start our pilgrimage with Jesus Christ and our fellow pilgrims. In time we learn to believe and discover the reality of the good news for ourselves. That is when we begin to write our own story of how God belongs to our life. This is our good news, our gospel; and we arrive at it by prayer.

This prayer book is a selection of prayers and reflections to be companions to your own thoughts and prayers. They follow the pattern given by Jesus, when he called himself 'the Way, the Truth and the Life' (John 14:6). My hope in offering these prayers to you is that they will give you support and encouragement as you raise your mind and heart to God.

✠ David Konstant
Bishop of Leeds
May 1996

INTRODUCTION

The apostles watched Jesus praying and were so moved by what they saw that they said: 'Lord, teach us to pray.' He said to them,

> 'Say this when you pray:
> Father, may your name be held holy,
> your kingdom come;
> give us each day our daily bread,
> and forgive us our sins,
> for we ourselves forgive each one
> who is in debt to us,
> And do not put us to the test.'
> *Luke 11:2–4*

Jesus urged his friends to pray: in the privacy of their rooms; together, where a few were assembled in his name; without babbling, but urgently, insistently, with confidence and joy, generously, openly, hopefully, always giving praise to God, and always listening to him. We are his friends, and so we too pray, each in our own way.

Sometimes we may feel the urge to express our prayer in words; at other times we may find that by repeating a word or phrase (like, 'Come, Lord Jesus') we are soon absorbed in

God's presence; or perhaps it will be enough for us on occasion to be quite still and know that God enfolds us.

Words, though, are almost always the beginning of our daily prayer. So here are some words that may help us to find God. They are pointers to prayer. Some are the words of the Old Testament psalmist; some are Jesus's own words; some are from the early followers of Jesus; there are prayers hallowed by the Church; and there are words of ordinary people, who in their own way have spoken to God. If they help us in our turn to find God at odd moments of the day, these words have done their work and will not return to him empty handed.

God approaches us through all our senses. So there are many things apart from words that may lead us to prayer. Music, beauty, even something as indefinable as atmosphere, can help us raise our minds and hearts to God. These may provoke us to prayer, accompany the written word, or stand on their own as a silent meditation on God's work.

We begin our day remembering God's continual presence, and we end the day trustfully, putting ourselves in his hands. In between times, alone or with others, we may turn to him in adoration, in praise, as petitioners, as sinners. Always we may be sure that he hears and answers our prayers.

✠

THE WAY, THE TRUTH, THE LIFE

Come, my Way, my Truth, my Life:
Such a Way as gives us breath:
Such a Truth as ends all strife:
Such a Life as killeth death.
George Herbert

O Lord Jesus Christ, who art the Way, the Truth, and the Life, we pray thee suffer us not to stray from thee who art the Way, nor to distrust thee who art the Truth, nor to rest in any other thing than thee, who art the Life. Teach us by thy Holy Spirit what to believe, what to do and wherein to take our rest. Amen.
Erasmus

Lord Jesus Christ, Son of the living God,
teach us to walk in your Way more trustfully,
to accept your Truth more faithfully,
and to share your Life more lovingly.
By the power of the Holy Spirit
help us in our work for the Church
so that we may come as one family
to the kingdom of the Father,
where you live for ever and ever.   Amen.
Congress Prayer

✠

MORNING PRAYER

If we are to remain close to God as to a friend, we need, at certain times of the day, to greet him and to listen to him. When we wake in the morning, and before we go to sleep at night, are good moments to place ourselves in his presence and to be still with him.

The sign of the cross

In the name of the Father,
and of the Son,
and of the Holy Spirit.   Amen.

Remember that God is present.

I am here and I call, you will hear me, O God.
Turn your ear to me; hear my words.

Psalm 16 (17):6

Pause for a moment's silent prayer of adoration.

A prayer of praise and thanks

How great is your name, O Lord our God,
through all the earth!

Your majesty is praised above the heavens;
on the lips of children and of babes
you have found praise to foil your enemy,
to silence the foe and the rebel.

When I see the heavens, the work of your hands,
the moon and the stars which you arranged,
what is man that you should keep him in mind,
mortal man that you care for him?

Yet you have made him little less than a god;
with glory and honour you crowned him,
gave him power over the works of your hand,
put all things under his feet.

All of them, sheep and cattle,
yes, even the savage beasts,
birds of the air, and fish
that make their way through the waters.

How great is your name, O Lord our God,
through all the earth!

Psalm 8

The apostles asked Jesus to teach them to pray; he teaches
us the same prayer to God who is our Father:

Our Father, who art in heaven,
hallowed be thy name;
thy kingdom come;
thy will be done on earth as it is in heaven.
Give us this day our daily bread;

and forgive us our trespasses
as we forgive those who trespass against us;
and lead us not into temptation,
but deliver us from evil.   Amen.

Pause for a moment's silent reflection; remember those
whose forgiveness we need, and those whom we must
forgive; remember the blessings that are our daily bread –
family, friends, work, leisure, home, happiness – and thank
God; remember the hardships and temptations of daily life,
and pray for strength and perseverance.

A prayer of self-giving for the day's work

Lord God,
you have brought me to a new day.
Give me grace today to work for your glory,
and for my neighbour's good;
so that all I say and do,
and think and pray,
may make this day a perfect gift.   Amen.

A prayer of confidence to the God who always cares

The Lord is my shepherd;
there is nothing I shall want.
Fresh and green are the pastures
where he gives me repose.
Near restful waters he leads me,
to revive my drooping spirit.

He guides me along the right path:
he is true to his name.
If I should walk in the valley of darkness
no evil would I fear.
You are there with your crook and your staff;
with these you give me comfort.

You have prepared a banquet for me
in the sight of my foes.
My head you have anointed with oil;
my cup is overflowing.

Surely goodness and kindness shall follow me
all the days of my life.
In the Lord's own house shall I dwell
for ever and ever.

Psalm 22 (23)

Some prayers for the day

* I praise and thank you, Lord, for your goodness to me.
Stay always close to me.

* Lord, you know me through and through.
Forgive my sins;
give me the grace to choose the better way.

* Lord, I believe in you;
increase my faith.

* Lord, I hope in you;
be a friend to me.

* Lord, I love you;
 show me how to live.

We may pause to pray for those we love and those who are
in need.

Remember now that we belong to the whole family of God,
and ask all the saints to pray for us and with us. Mary is the
first of all the saints and so we pray:

> Hail Mary, full of grace, the Lord is with thee.
> Blessed art thou among women,
> and blessed is the fruit of thy womb, Jesus.
> Holy Mary, mother of God, pray for us sinners
> now and at the hour of our death.   Amen.

Finally, as we begin the day's work, we may praise God
again in the words of a familiar prayer:

> Glory be to the Father,
> and to the Son,
> and to the Holy Spirit;
> as it was in the beginning
> is now and ever shall be,
> world without end.   Amen.

JESUS CHRIST, THE WAY

The Lord guides the steps of a man
and makes safe the path of one he loves.
Though he stumble he shall never fall
for the Lord holds him by the hand.
                    Psalm 36(37):23–24

Jesus invites us, like the apostles, to listen to his call and to follow him; to be his disciples; to learn that leadership demands service; to walk the way of self-denial, of poverty and of obedience; to come to him in our sickness, our anger and our sinfulness; to pray; to be unworried; to work confidently and to live peaceably in our homes so as to be happy with him for ever.

VOCATION

God has created me to do him some definite service. He has committed some work to me which he has not committed to another. I have my mission – I may never know it in this life, but I shall be told it in the next.

I am a link in a chain, a bond of connexion between persons. He has not created me for naught. I shall do good, I shall do his work. I shall be an angel of peace, a preacher of truth in my own place while not intending it – if I do but keep his commandments.

Therefore I will trust him. Whatever, wherever I am. I can never be thrown away. If I am in sickness, my sickness may serve him; in perplexity, my perplexity may serve him; if I am in sorrow, my sorrow may serve him. He does nothing in vain. He knows what he is about. He may take away my friends, he may throw me among strangers. He may make me feel desolate, make my spirits sink, hide my future from me – still he knows what he is about.

Cardinal Newman

Lord, give courage and strength to the young. Help them to choose their work and make the right decisions for their way of life.

Bidding Prayer

Brothers, you have been called and chosen: work all the harder to justify it. In this way you will be granted admittance into the eternal kingdom of our Lord and Saviour Jesus Christ.

2 Peter 1:10–11

We have been enlightened by Christ.
We are to walk always as children of the light.
May we keep the flame of faith alive in our hearts.
When the Lord comes,
may he go out to meet us with all the saints in the heavenly kingdom.

From the Baptismal Service

DISCIPLESHIP

Christ be near at either hand,
Christ behind, before me stand,
Christ with me where e'er I go,
Christ around, above, below.

Christ be in my heart and mind,
Christ within my soul enshrined,
Christ control my wayward heart;
Christ abide and ne'er depart.

Christ my life and only Way.
Christ my lantern night and day;
Christ be my unchanging friend,
Guide and Shepherd to the end.

tr. J Fennelly

The Lord says: 'Which is the good way? Take it then, and
you shall find rest.'

Jeremiah 6:16

Free your minds, then, of encumbrances; control them,
and put your trust in nothing but the grace that will be
given you when Jesus Christ is revealed. Do not behave
in the way that you liked to before you learnt the truth;
make a habit of obedience; be holy in all you do, since it
is the Holy One who has called you, and scripture says,
'Be holy, for I am holy'.

1 Peter 1:13–16

As he was walking on he saw Levi, the son of Alphaeus, sitting by the counting house, and he said to him, 'Follow me'. And he got up and followed him.

Mark 2:14

Someone said to Jesus, 'I will follow you, sir, but first let me go and say good-bye to my people at home.' Jesus said to him, 'Once the hand is laid on the plough, no one who looks back is fit for the kingdom of God.'

Luke 9:61–62

'What about us?' Peter asked Jesus, 'We have left everything and followed you.' Jesus said, 'I tell you solemnly, there is no one who has left house, brothers, sisters, father, children or land for my sake and for the sake of the gospel who will not be repaid a hundred times over … and in the world to come, eternal life.'

Mark 10:28–30

Come to me, all you who labour and are overburdened, and I will give you rest. Shoulder my yoke and learn from me, for I am gentle and humble in heart, and you will find rest for your souls. Yes, my yoke is easy, and my burden light.

Matthew 11:28–30

The disciple is not superior to his teacher, nor the slave to his master. It is enough for the disciple that he should grow to be like his teacher, and the slave like his master.

Matthew 10:24–25

In your minds you must be the same as Christ Jesus.

Philippians 2:5

Lord, I give you today my prayers, thoughts, works, sufferings and joys, that they may be for your glory and for the good of the world.

A Morning Offering

Jesu, blessed Jesu, strengthen me in soul and body, that I may not fail you.

St John Paine

Jesus said:
    'I am the light of the world;
    anyone who follows me will not be walking in the dark;
    he will have the Light of Life.'

John 8:12

Lord Jesus,
I give you my hands to do your work.
I give you my feet to go your way.
I give you my eyes to see as you do.
I give you my tongue to speak your words.
I give you my mind that you may think in me.
I give you my spirit that you may pray in me.
Above all, I give you my heart
that you may love in me your Father and all mankind.
I give you my whole self that you may grow in me,
so that it is you, Lord Jesus,
who live and work and pray in me.

Grail Prayer

LEADERSHIP

The greatest among you must be your servant. Anyone who exalts himself will be humbled, and anyone who humbles himself will be exalted.

Matthew 23:11–12

Anyone who wants to become great among you must be your servant, and anyone who wants to be first among you must be slave to all. For the Son of Man himself did not come to be served, but to serve, and to give his life as a ransom for many.

Mark 10:44–45

The Lord carried you as a man carries his child, all along the road you travelled.

Deuteronomy 1:31

Since in Jesus, the Son of God, we have the supreme high priest who has gone through to the highest heaven, we must never let go of the faith that we have professed. For it is not as if we have a high priest who was incapable of feeling our weaknesses with us; but we have one who has been tempted in every way that we are, though he is without sin. Let us be confident, then, in approaching the throne of grace, that we shall have mercy from him and find grace when we are in need of help.

Hebrews 4:15–16

I led you with reins of kindness,
with leading strings of love.

Hosea 11:3

Let us not lose sight of Jesus, who leads us in our faith and brings it to perfection: for the sake of the joy which was still in the future, he endured the cross, disregarding the shamefulness of it, and from now on has taken his place at the right of God's throne.

Hebrews 12:2

SERVICE

Teach us, good Lord,
to serve you as you deserve;
to give and not to count the cost,
to fight and not to heed the wounds,
to toil and not to seek for rest,
to labour and not to ask for any reward,
save that of knowing that we do your will;
through Jesus Christ our Lord.   Amen.

St Ignatius

What does the Lord your God ask of you? Only this: to fear the Lord your God, to follow all his ways, to love him, to serve the Lord your God with all your heart and all your soul.

Deuteronomy 10:12

Repay no one evil for evil. If your enemy is hungry, feed him; if he is thirsty, give him drink. Do not be overcome by evil, but overcome evil with good.

from *Romans 12:17–21*

I was hungry and you gave me food.
  Blessed be God for ever.

I was thirsty and you gave me drink.
  Blessed be God for ever.
I was a stranger and you made me welcome.
  Blessed be God for ever.
I was naked and you clothed me.
  Blessed be God for ever.
I was sick and you visited me.
  Blessed be God for ever.
I was in prison and you came to see me.
  Blessed be God for ever.

from Matthew 25

There is a variety of gifts but always the same Spirit; there are all sorts of service to be done, but always to the same Lord; working in all sorts of different ways in different people, it is the same God who is working in all of them.

1 Corinthians 12:4–6

The greatest among you must behave as if he were the youngest, the leader as if he were the one who serves. For who is the greater: the one at table, or the one who serves? The one at table, surely? Yet here am I among you as one who serves!

Luke 22:27

I tell you most solemnly, no servant is greater than his master, no messenger is greater than the man who sent him.

John 13:16

Each one of you has received a special grace, so, like stewards responsible for all these different graces of God, put yourselves at the service of others. If you are a speaker, speak in words that seem to come from God; if you are a helper, help as though every action was done at God's orders; so that in everything God may receive the glory, through Jesus Christ, since to him alone belong all glory and power for ever and ever.

1 Peter 4:10–11

Make us worthy, Lord,
to serve our fellow men throughout the world,
who live and die in poverty and hunger.
Give them by our hands
this day their daily bread,
and by our understanding love
give peace and joy.

Pope Paul VI

SELF-DENIAL

Jesus said to his disciples, 'If anyone wants to be a follower of mine, let him renounce himself, and take up his cross and follow me. For anyone who wants to save his life will lose it; but anyone who loses his life for my sake will find it. What, then, will a man gain if he wins the whole world and ruins his life?'

Matthew 16:24–26

Jesus said:
'Unless a grain of wheat falls on the ground and dies,
it remains only a single grain;
but if it dies, it yields a rich harvest.'

John 12:24

He was obedient unto death, even to death on a cross.

Philippians 2:8

'It makes me happy to suffer for you,' writes St Paul, 'as I am suffering now, and in my own body to do what I can to make up all that has still to be undergone by Christ, for the sake of his body, the Church.'

Colossians 1:24

O blessed Jesu, make me understand and remember that whatsoever we gain, if we lose you, all is lost, and whatsoever we lose, if we gain you, all is gained.

St Thomas Cottam

POVERTY

Happy you who are poor: yours is the kingdom of God. Alas for you who are rich: you are having your consolation now.

Luke 6:20, 24

Give your bread to those who are hungry, and your clothes to those who are naked. Whatever you own in plenty, devote a proportion to almsgiving; and when you give alms do not do it grudgingly.

Tobit 4:16–17

O, come to the water all you who are thirsty;
though you have no money, come!
Buy corn without money, and eat,
and, at no cost, wine and milk.

Isaiah 55:1

O Lord Jesus Christ, take as your right, receive as my gift, all my liberty, my memory, my understanding, my will; all that I have, all that I am, all that I can be. To you, O Lord, I restore it, all is yours, dispose of it according to your will. Give me your love. Give me your grace. It is enough for me.

St Ignatius

Jesus was setting out on a journey when a man ran up, knelt before him and put this question to him, 'Good master, what must I do to inherit eternal life?' ... Jesus looked steadily at him and loved him, and said, 'There is one thing you lack. Go and sell everything you own, and give the money to the poor, and you will have treasure in heaven; then come, follow me.' But his face fell at these words, and he went away sad, for he was a man of great wealth.

Mark 10:17–22

Two mites, two drops (yet all her house and land),
Falls from a steady heart, though trembling hand.
The other's wanton wealth foams high and brave,
The other cast away, she only gave.

Richard Crashaw

A cheerful giver does not count the cost of what he gives. His heart is set on pleasing and cheering him to whom the gift is given.

Julian of Norwich

Jesus said to his disciples, 'I tell you solemnly, it will be hard for a rich man to enter the kingdom of heaven.'

Matthew 19:23

OBEDIENCE

We should rather love obedience than fear disobedience.

St Francis de Sales

You have been obedient to the truth and purified your souls until you can love like brothers in sincerity; let your love for each other be real and from the heart – your new birth was not from any mortal seed but from the everlasting word of the living and everlasting God. What is this word? It is the good news that has been brought to you.

1 Peter 1:22–25

Almighty, ever-living God,
make us ever obey you willingly and promptly.
Teach us how to serve you
with sincere and upright hearts
in every sphere of life.

The Prayer of the Church

Be strong and show yourself a man. Observe the injunctions of the Lord your God, following his ways and keeping his laws, that so you may be successful in all you do and undertake.

1 Kings 2:2–3

No man securely commands but he who has learned to obey.

Thomas à Kempis

I pray that the God of peace, who brought our Lord Jesus back from the dead, may make you ready to do his will in any kind of good action.

Hebrews 13:20–21

It is not those who say to me, 'Lord, Lord', who will enter the kingdom of heaven, but the person who does the will of my Father in heaven.

Matthew 7:21

Jesus said:
 'My food
 is to do the will of the one who sent me,
 and to complete his work.'

John 4:34

ANGER

In spite of your anger, Lord, have compassion.

Habbakuk 3:4

Happy the gentle:
they shall have the earth for their heritage.

Matthew 5:4

Let your words be for the improvement of others, as occasion offers, and do good to your listeners, otherwise you will only be grieving the Holy Spirit of God who has marked you with his seal for you to be set free when the day comes. Never have grudges against others, or lose your temper, or raise your voice to anybody, or call each other names, or allow any sort of spitefulness. Be friends with one another, and kind, forgiving each other as readily as God forgave you in Christ.

Ephesians 4:29–32

Remember this, my dear brothers: be quick to listen but slow to speak and slow to rouse your temper; God's righteousness is never served by man's anger. Nobody must imagine that he is religious while he still goes on deceiving himself and not keeping control over his tongue; anyone who does this has the wrong idea of religion.

James 1:19–20, 26

I saw full surely that wherever our Lord appears, peace reigns, and anger has no place. For I saw no whit of anger in God.

Julian of Norwich

Come back to me with all your heart …
Turn to the Lord your God again,
for he is all tenderness and compassion,
slow to anger, rich in graciousness,
and ready to relent.

Joel 2:12–13

SORROW

God of mercy and compassion,
slow to anger, O Lord,
abounding in love and truth,
turn and take pity on me.

Psalm 85:15–16

A leper came to Jesus and pleaded on his knees: 'If you want to,' he said, 'you can cure me.' Feeling sorry for him Jesus stretched out his hand and touched him. 'Of course I want to!' he said. 'Be cured!' And the leprosy left him at once and he was cured.

Mark 1:14

My God, I am sorry and ask forgiveness for my sins.
By the help of your grace I will try not to sin again.
An Act of Contrition

Naked I came from my mother's womb,
naked I shall return.
The Lord gave, the Lord has taken back.
Blessed be the name of the Lord!

If we take happiness from God's hand, must we not take sorrow too?

Job 1:21, 2:10

Jesus Christ, our Saviour, you were like us in all things but sin. Be with me when I am tempted, and stay with me when I fall, so that by your grace I may learn to trust in your strength.   Amen.

Lord Jesus Christ, Son of God
have mercy on me, a sinner.

cf. Luke 18:13

Almighty, ever-living God,
whose love surpasses all that we ask or deserve,
open up for us the treasures of your mercy.

Forgive us all that weighs on our conscience,
and grant us more even than we dare to ask.
We make our prayer through Christ our Lord.   Amen.

A Sunday Prayer

Lord God,
in your goodness have mercy on me:
do not look on my sins,
but take away my guilt.
Create in me a clean heart
and renew within me an upright spirit.

PRAYER

Seek the Lord and he will give life to your soul.

Where two or three meet in my name, I shall be there
with them.

Matthew 18:20

To seek God
means first of all
to let yourself be found by him.
He is the God of Abraham, Isaac, and Jacob.
He is the God of Jesus Christ.
He is your God,
not because he is yours, but because you are his.

Rule for a New Brother

When you pray, go to your private room and, when you have shut your door, pray to your Father who is in that secret place, and your Father who sees all that is done in secret will reward you.

Matthew 6:6

Like the deer that yearns
for running streams,
so my soul is yearning
for you my God.

Psalm 41(42):1

You should be awake, and praying not to be put to the test. The spirit is willing, but the flesh is weak.

Mark 14:38

Ask and it will be given to you; search, and you will find; knock, and the door will be opened to you. For the one who asks always receives; the one who searches always finds; the one who knocks will always have the door opened to him ... If you who are evil, know how to give your children what is good, how much more will your Father in heaven give good things to those who ask him!

Matthew 7:7–11

My eyes watch for you before dawn.

from *Psalm 118(119):148*

Ask and you will receive, and so your joy will be complete.

John 16:24

We fly to thy patronage,
O holy Mother of God;
Despise not our petitions in our necessities,
but deliver us always from all dangers,
O glorious and blessed virgin.

Traditional

I called with all my heart; Lord, hear me.

ANXIETY

Lord, listen to my cry,
for I am in the depths of distress.

Psalm 141(142):7

Does a woman forget her baby at the breast,
or fail to cherish the son of her womb?
Yet even if these forget,
I will never forget you, says the Lord God.

Isaiah 49:15

Jesus said: 'Come to me, all you who labour and are over-burdened, and I will give you rest. Shoulder my yoke and learn from me, for I am gentle and humble in heart, and you will find rest for your souls. Yes, my yoke is easy and my burden light.'

Matthew 11:28–30

Jesus said to his disciples: 'This is why I am telling you not to worry about your life and what you are to eat, nor about your body and how you are to clothe it. For life means more than food, and the body more than

24

clothing. There is no need to be afraid, little flock, for it has pleased your Father to give you the kingdom.'

Luke 12:22–23, 32

Blessed be the God and Father of our Lord Jesus Christ, a gentle Father and the God of all consolation, who comforts us in all our sorrows, so that we can offer others, in their sorrows, the consolation that we have received from God ourselves. Indeed, as the sufferings of Christ overflow to us, so, through Christ, does our consolation overflow.

2 Corinthians 1:3–5

I called to the Lord in my distress;
he answered and freed me.
The Lord is at my side, I do not fear.

Psalm 117(118):5–6

Deliver us, Lord, from every evil,
and grant us peace in our day.
In your mercy keep us free from sin
and protect us from all anxiety
as we wait in joyful hope
for the coming of our Saviour, Jesus Christ.   Amen.

A Prayer before Communion

Christ has said, 'My grace is enough for you, my power is at its best in weakness.' So I shall be very happy to make my weaknesses my special boast so that the power of Christ may stay over me, and that is why I am quite content with my weaknesses, and with insults, hardships, persecution, and the agonies I go through for Christ's sake. For it is when I am weak that I am strong.

2 Corinthians 12:9–10

FAMILY

Guard your family, Lord, with constant loving care
for in your divine grace we place our only hope.

The Prayer of the Church

Lord, bless the household of which I form a part. Show us how we can help one another, share our interests and sorrows and joys with one another, be ready to make sacrifices for one another. I ask that I may find my joy in serving them as you found your joy in serving Mary and Joseph on earth.

Hubert van Zeller

Jesus exclaimed, 'I bless you, Father, Lord of heaven and of earth, for hiding these things from the learned and the clever, and revealing them to mere children.'

Matthew 11:25

Jesus said, 'I tell you solemnly, unless you change and become like little children you will never enter the kingdom of heaven. And so, the one who makes himself as little as this little child will be the greatest in the kingdom of heaven.'

Matthew 18:3–4

Anyone who welcomes one of these little children in my name, welcomes me; and anyone who welcomes me welcomes not me but the one who sent me.

Mark 9:37

A wife should regard her husband as she regards Jesus Christ. Just as Christ is head of the Church and saves her, so is a husband the head of the family. A husband must love his wife just as Christ loved the Church and gave himself for her. Children have a duty to obey their parents. The commandment, 'Love your parents,' carries with it this promise, 'You will do well and live happily.' On their part, parents must never make their children resentful, but should bring them up, correct them, and guide them as the Lord does. Finally, grow strong in the Lord, with his strength. Pray all the time for whatever you need, under the guidance of the Holy Spirit.

from Ephesians 5 and 6

As long as we love one another
God will live in us,
and his love will be complete in us.

1 John 4:12

Out of his infinite glory, may the Father give you the power through his Spirit for your hidden self to grow strong, so that Christ may live in your hearts through faith, and then, planted in love and built on love, you will with all the saints have strength to grasp the breadth and the length, the height and the depth; until, knowing the love of Christ, which is beyond all knowledge, you are filled with the utter fulness of God.

Ephesians 3:16–19

THE DAY'S WORK

When I see the heavens, the work of your hands,
the moon and the stars which you arranged
what is man that you should keep him in mind,
mortal man that you care for him?
Yet you have made him little less than a god;
with glory and honour you crowned him,
gave him power over the works of your hand,
put all things under his feet.

Psalm 8:4–7

Don't delude yourself into thinking that God can be
cheated: where a man sows, there he reaps: if he sows in
the field of self-indulgence he will get a harvest of cor-
ruption out of it; if he sows in the field of the Spirit he
will get from it a harvest of eternal life. We must never
get tired of doing good because if we don't give up the
struggle we shall get our harvest at the proper time.
While we have the chance, we must do good to all, and
especially to our brothers in the faith.

Galatians 6:7–10

We beg you to pay proper respect to those who work
with you, those whom the Lord has chosen to guide and
instruct you. Treat them with the greatest respect and
love, because of the work they do. Be at peace among
yourselves.

1 Thessalonians 5:12–13

Lord, be the beginning and end
of all that we do and say.

Prompt our actions with your grace
and complete them with your all-powerful help.
Through Christ our Lord.   Amen.

A Sunday Prayer

Father, I dedicate this new day to you;
as I go about my work, I ask you to bless those I come into
    contact with.
Lord, I pray for all men and women who work to earn
    their living;
give them satisfaction in what they do.
Spirit of God, comfort the unemployed and their families;
they are your children and my brothers and sisters.
I ask you to help them find work soon.

A Morning Prayer

Teach us, good Lord, to serve you as you deserve;
to give and not to count the cost;
to fight and not to heed the wounds;
to toil and not to seek for rest;
to labour and to ask for no reward,
save that of knowing that we do your will;
through Christ our Lord.

St Ignatius

God, Lord and Master of the vineyard,
you allot us our task,
and determine the just rewards of our labours.
Help us to bear the burden of the day
and accept your will in all things without complaint.
Through Christ our Lord.   Amen.

The Prayer of the Church

Blessed are you, Lord God of all creation,
through your goodness we enjoy those things
that are the fruits of the earth and the work of our hands,
may they be for us a source of lasting life.
Blessed be God for ever.

An Offertory Prayer

✠

JESUS CHRIST, THE TRUTH

In the beginning was the Word
the Word was with God
and the Word was God.

John 1:1

Truth is eternal and unchanging. 'Your truth, O Lord,
will last from age to age.' Jesus promised to send his Spirit to lead us to all truth. This truth is the ground of our
faith, the source of self-knowledge, the beginning of forgiveness and healing, the basis of justice and of peace; it
is the cause of our joy; it is expressed in law; it is the only
true foundation of unity.

SPIRIT

I shall ask the Father,
and he will give you another Advocate
to be with you for ever,
the Spirit of Truth.
The Advocate, the Holy Spirit,
whom the Father will send in my name,
will teach you everything
and remind you of all I have said to you.

John 14:16–17, 26

Your body, you know, is the temple of the Holy Spirit, who is in you since you received him from God. That is why you should use your body for the glory of God.

1 Corinthians 6:19–20

I shall give you a new heart, and put a new spirit in you; I shall remove the heart of stone from your bodies and give you a heart of flesh instead. I shall put my Spirit in you, and make you keep my laws and sincerely respect my observances. You shall be my people and I will be your God.

Ezekiel 36:25–27

In the one Spirit we were all baptised.

1 Corinthians 12:13

Everyone moved by the Spirit is a son of God. The Spirit you received is not the spirit of slaves bringing fear into your lives again; it is the spirit of sons, and it makes us cry out, 'Abba, Father!'. The Spirit himself and our spirit bear united witness that we are children of God.

The Spirit too comes to help us in our weakness. For when we cannot choose words in order to pray properly, the Spirit himself expresses our plea in a way that could never be put into words, and God who knows everything in our hearts knows perfectly well what he means, and that the pleas of the saints expressed by the Spirit are according to the mind of God.

Romans 8:14–16, 26–27

Holy Spirit of God, sent by the Father and the Son, fill my heart with your love. Lead me to know myself, to root out my selfishness, and to share with others the fruits of your presence: love, joy, peace, patience, kindness, goodness, trustfulness, gentleness and self-control.

cf. Galatians 5:22

FAITH

In God alone is my soul at rest;
my help comes from him.
He alone is my rock, my stronghold,
my fortress: I stand firm.

Psalm 61(62):2–3

Jesus said: 'I tell you solemnly, if your faith were the size of a mustard seed you could say to this mountain, "Move from here to there," and it would move; nothing would be impossible for you.'

Matthew 17:20–21

Jesus said:
'I am the resurrection.
If anyone believes in me, even though he dies he will live
and whoever lives and believes in me
will never die.'

John 11:25–26

Jesus said: 'Doubt no longer but believe.' Thomas replied, 'My Lord and my God.' Jesus said to him, 'You believe because you can see. Happy are those who have not seen and yet believe.'

John 20:27–29

Jesus said: 'If anyone declares himself for me in the presence of men, I will declare myself for him in the presence of my Father in heaven. But the one who disowns me in the presence of men, I will disown him in the presence of my Father in heaven.'

Matthew 10:32–33

Lord I believe! Help what little faith I have.

Mark 9:25

By whatever means he teaches us, his will is that we perceive him wisely, receive him joyfully, and keep ourselves in him faithfully.

Julian of Norwich

Be calm but vigilant, because your enemy the devil is prowling round like a roaring lion, looking for someone to eat. Stand up to him, strong in faith and in the knowledge that your brothers all over the world are suffering the same things. You will have to suffer only for a little while. The God of all grace will see that all is well again; he will confirm, strengthen and support you. His power lasts for ever and ever.   Amen.

1 Peter 5:8–11

Your word is a lamp for my steps and a light for my path.

Psalm 18(119):105

We have never failed to remember you in our prayers and to give thanks for you to God, the Father of our Lord Jesus Christ, ever since we heard about your faith in Christ Jesus and the love that you show towards all the saints because of the hope which is stored up for you in heaven.

Colossians 1:3–4

O my God, I believe in you, and all that your Church teaches, because you have said it, and your word is true.

An Act of Faith

Lord God,
since by the adoption of grace
you have made us children of light:
do not let false doctrine darken our minds,
but grant that your light may shine within us
and we may always live in the brightness of truth.

A Sunday Prayer

It is by grace that you have been saved, through faith; not by anything of your own, but by a gift from God. We are God's work of art, created in Christ Jesus to live the good life as from the beginning he had meant us to live it.

Ephesians 2:8–10

I believe in God, the Father Almighty,
creator of heaven and earth;
and in Jesus Christ, his only Son, our Lord;
who was conceived by the Holy Spirit,
born of the Virgin Mary,
suffered under Pontius Pilate,
was crucified, died and was buried.
He descended into hell;
the third day he rose again from the dead.

He ascended into heaven
and sits at the right hand of God the almighty Father.
From thence he will come to judge the living and the dead.
I believe in the Holy Spirit;
the holy catholic Church;
the communion of saints;
the forgiveness of sins;
the resurrection of the body;
and the life everlasting.   Amen.

The Apostles' Creed

HUMILITY

Wrap yourselves in humility to be servants of each other,
because God refuses the proud and will always favour the
humble. Bow down, then, before the power of God now,
and he will raise you up on the appointed day.

1 Peter 5:5–6

In your minds you must be the same as Christ Jesus:
His state was divine,
yet he did not cling
to his equality with God
but emptied himself
to assume the condition of a slave,
and became as men are;
and being as all men are;
he was humbler yet,
even to accepting death,
death on a cross.
But God raised him high
and gave him the name

which is above all other names
so that all beings
in the heavens, on earth and in the underworld,
should bend the knee at the name of Jesus
and that every tongue should acclaim
Jesus Christ as Lord
to the glory of God the Father.

Philippians 2:6–11

The Lord guides the humble in the right path.

cf. Psalm 24(25):9

Unless you become like little children you will not enter
into the kingdom of heaven.

Matthew 18:3

Learn from me, for I am gentle and humble in heart.

Matthew 11:29

God does not see as man sees; man looks at appearances
but the Lord looks at the heart.

1 Samuel 16:7

My soul glorifies the Lord,
my spirit rejoices in God, my saviour.
He looks on his servant in her lowliness;
henceforth all ages will call me blessed.

The Almighty works marvels for me.
Holy his name!
His mercy is from age to age,
on those who fear him.

He puts forth his arm in strength
and scatters the proud-hearted.
He casts the mighty from their thrones
and raises the lowly.

He fills the starving with good things,
and sends the rich away empty.

He protects Israel, his servant,
remembering his mercy,
the mercy promised to our fathers,
to Abraham and his sons for ever.

The Magnificat

The first degree of humility is obedience without delay.

St Benedict

In all my walks it seems to me
that the grace of God lies in courtesy.

Hilaire Belloc

Almighty God, take from me all vainglorious thoughts, all
desires for mine own praise, all envy, covetousness, gluttony,
sloth and lechery, all wrathful affections, all desire for revenge,
all delight in harm to others, all pleasure in provoking them to
wrath and anger, all delight in upbraiding and insulting them in
their affliction and calamity. Give freely unto me, good Lord,
thy love and favour which my love for thee, be it ever so great,
could not receive except out of thine own great goodness.

St Thomas More

FORGIVENESS

Forgive us our trespasses,
as we forgive those who trespass against us.

The *Our Father*

Jesus said: 'If you forgive others their failings, your heavenly Father will forgive you yours, but if you do not forgive others, your Father will not forgive your failings either.'

Matthew 6:14–15

Then Peter came up to Jesus and said: 'Lord, how often must I forgive my brother if he wrongs me? As often as seven times?' Jesus answered, 'Not seven, I tell you, but seventy-seven times.'

Matthew 18:21–22

Jesus said: 'Be compassionate as your Father is compassionate.'

Luke 6:36

You are God's chosen race, his saints; he loves you, and you should be clothed in sincere compassion, in kindness and humility, gentleness and patience. Bear with one another; forgive each other as soon as a quarrel begins. The Lord has forgiven you; now you must do the same. Over all these clothes, to keep them together and complete them, put on love. And may the peace of Christ reign in your hearts, because it was for this that you were called together as parts of one body. Always be thankful.

Colossians 3:12–15

Father, forgive them; they do not know what they are doing.

Luke 23:34

Give me thy grace, good Lord:
to set the world at nought,
to set my mind fast upon thee,
and not to hang upon the blast of men's mouths.
To be content to be solitary.
Not to long for worldly company.
Little and little utterly to cast off the world,
and rid my mind of all the business thereof.
Not to long to hear of any worldly things.
But that the hearing of worldly phantasies
may be to me displeasant,
gladly to be thinking of God.
Piteously to call for his help.
To lean upon the comfort of God.
Busily to labour to love him.
To know mine own violence and wretchedness.
To humble myself under the mighty hand of God.
To bewail my sins passed.
For the purging of them patiently to suffer adversity.
Gladly to bear my purgatory here.
To be joyful of tribulations.

St Thomas More

Heal my soul for I have sinned against you.

cf. Psalm 40(41):4

Grant me, O God, so worthily to receive this most holy body and blood of thy Son that I may thereby receive the forgiveness of all my sins, be filled with thy Holy Spirit, and find peace. For thou only art God and there is no other besides thee.

The Sarum Missal

To those who love you, Lord,
you promise to come with your Son
and make your home within them.
Come then with your purifying grace
and make our hearts a place where you can dwell.

A Sunday Prayer

Look in love on all whose sins have separated them from
    you.
Reconcile them to yourself and to your Church.

Bidding Prayer

Cry wrenched wrung wounded radiant hearts,
   'O Christ, forgive!'
Beg nailed gnarled bloodied Christened hands,
   'Dear Jesu, bless!'
Smile blind burnt sunken glowing eyes,
   'Have mercy, Lord!'
Plead toiled torn aching tempered frames,
   'Sweet Master, save!'

DK

Holy Father,
you know both our strength and our weakness.
Help us to know ourselves better
so that we will always judge ourselves
honestly and openly.

May we be guided by your Holy Spirit
who with you and your Son
is the source of all love and knowledge.

A Prayer for Confession

Never grow tired of what is right.

2 Thessalonians 3:13

Enlighten our minds, O God, and purify our desires. Correct our wanderings and pardon our defects, so that by thy guidance we may be preserved from making shipwreck of our faith, be kept in a good conscience, and at length be landed in the safe haven of eternal peace. Through Jesus Christ our Lord.   Amen.

St Anselm

HEALING

The Son of Man has come to seek out and save what was lost.

Luke 19:10

Come to me all you who labour and are overburdened, and I will give you rest. Shoulder my yoke and learn from me, for I am gentle and humble in heart, and you will find rest for your souls. Yes, my yoke is easy and my burden light.

Matthew 11:28–30

I tell you that her sins, her many sins, must have been forgiven her, or she would not have shown such great love. It is the man who is forgiven little who shows little love ... Your faith has saved you; go in peace.

Luke 7:47–50

Help us, O Lord our God, since we cannot flee from the body, or the body flee from us. We must needs carry about the body, because it is bound up with us. We cannot destroy it; we are forced to preserve it. But the world surrounds us and assails us through the five gateways of sense.

St Bernard

O Lord, I cried to you for help and you have healed me.
I will thank you for ever.

Psalm 29(30):3, 13

Lord, support us as we pray,
protect us day and night,
so that we who under your guiding hand
live in a world of change,
may always draw strength from you,
with whom there is no shadow of alteration.

Evening Prayer

I lift up my eyes to the mountains;
from where shall come my help?
My help shall come from the Lord
who made heaven and earth.

Psalm 120(121):1–2

JUSTICE

Justice and right are the pillars of your throne, O Lord,
love and truth walk in your presence.

Psalm 88(89):15

Jesus said to the rich young man: 'There is still one thing you lack. Sell all that you own and distribute the money to the poor, and you will have treasure in heaven; then come, follow me.'

Luke 18:22

'Blessed are those who hunger and thirst for justice: they shall have their fill.'

Matthew 5:6

Almighty Father, bring justice to our world, that your people may live in the joy of your peace.

Bidding Prayer

This is what the Lord asks of you:
only this, to act justly,
to love tenderly,
and to walk humbly with your God.

Micah 6:8

If a man who was rich enough in this world's goods
saw that one of his brothers was in need,
but closed his heart to him,
how could the love of God live in him?
My children,
our love is not to be just words or mere talk,
but something real and active.

1 John 3:17–18

Do not be afraid of any man, for the judgement is God's.

Deuteronomy 1:17

Lord, make me an instrument of your peace:
Where there is hatred, let me sow love;
where there is injury, let me sow pardon;
where there is doubt, let me sow faith;
where there is despair, let me give hope;
where there is darkness, let me give light;
where there is sadness, let me give joy.

O Divine Master, grant that I may try
    not to be comforted, but to comfort;
    not to be understood, but to understand;
    not to be loved, but to love.
Because it is in giving that we receive,
it is in forgiving that we are forgiven,
and it is in dying that we are born to eternal life.

St Francis of Assisi

True Light of the World, Lord Jesus Christ,
as you enlighten all people for their salvation,
give us grace, we pray,
to herald your coming
by preparing the ways of justice and of peace.

Morning Prayer

PEACE

Truly I have set my soul in silence and peace.
A weaned child on its mother's breast even so is my soul.

Psalm 130(131):2

May the Lord of peace himself give you peace all the time and in every way.

2 Thessalonians 3:16

He was pierced through for our faults, crushed for our sins.
On him lies a punishment that brings us peace,
and through his wounds we are healed.

Isaiah 53:6

Be at peace, and know that nothing can separate you from the love of God made visible in Christ Jesus our Lord.

Romans 8:39

Jesus came and stood among them. 'Peace be with you,' he said to them. The disciples were filled with joy when they saw the Lord, and he said to them again, 'Peace be with you.'

John 20:20–21

Lord Jesus Christ, you said to your apostles:
'I leave you peace, my peace I give you.'
Look not on our sins, but on the faith of your Church,
and grant us the peace and unity of your kingdom
where you live for ever and ever.   Amen.

A Prayer before Communion

Guide our steps, good Lord, in the ways of your service, and forgive us our sins, that we may discover the gift of your peace and share it with others.

The Prayer of the Church

Blessed are the peacemakers, they shall be called the sons of God.

Matthew 6:9

Deep peace of the running wave to you.
Deep peace of the flowing air to you.
Deep peace of the quiet earth to you.
Deep peace of the shining stars to you.
Deep peace of the Son of Peace to you.

Irish Blessing

There is no need to worry; but if there is anything you need, pray for it, asking God for it with prayer and thanksgiving, and that peace of God, which is so much greater than we can understand, will guard your hearts and your thoughts, in Christ Jesus. Then the God of peace will be with you.

Philippians 4:6–9

The soul is immediately at one with God, when it is truly at peace in itself.

Julian of Norwich

Give us perfect peace, Lord,
so that we may delight in serving you,
all the days of our life,
and at the last, with our Lady's help,
come safely to your presence.

Midday Prayer

Lord, give peace to our troubled world; and give to your children security of mind and freedom from anxiety.

Bidding Prayer

JOY

Like the deer that yearns
for running streams,
so my soul is yearning
for you, my God.

Psalm 41(42):2

Jesus said:
'You are sad now, but I shall see you again,
and your hearts will be full of joy,
and that joy no one shall take from you.'

John 16:22

Be happy at all times; pray constantly; and for all things give thanks to God, because this is what God expects you to do in Christ Jesus.

1 Thessalonians 13:16–18

Fixing his eyes on his disciples Jesus said:
'How happy are you who are poor,
yours is the kingdom of God.
Happy you who are hungry now, you shall be satisfied.
Happy you who weep now, you shall laugh.'

Luke 6:20–21

Rejoice in the Lord always, and again I say rejoice.

Philippians 4:4

My heart rejoices, my soul is glad;
even my body shall rest in safety.
You will show me the path of life,
the fulness of joy in your presence,
at your right hand happiness for ever.

Psalm 15(16):9–11

If you abide in love
you will abide in God
and not wander any more in darkness.

Then live in joyfulness and hope
unanxious, without any trace of fear,
at peace with yourself and the world,
in ceaseless reverence and thanks.
Because God's love for you endures for ever.

Rule for a New Brother

Lord God,
you are the source of all that is good,
of all that brings joy.
Help us to rejoice always in you
and to share our joy with others.

The Prayer of the Church

He will never have full joy in us until we have full joy in him,
truly seeing his lovely blessed face.

Julian of Norwich

LAW

'Heaven and earth will pass away but my words will not pass away,' says the Lord.

Matthew 24:35

Let your love come and I shall live,
for your law is my delight.

Psalm 118(119):77

May your hearts be wholly with the Lord our God,
following his laws and keeping his commandments.

1 Kings 8:61

A wise man will not hate the law,
but he who is hypocritical about it
is like a boat in a storm.

Ecclesiasticus 33:2

Avoid getting into debt, except the debt of mutual love. If you love your fellow men you have carried out your obligation. All the commandments are summed up in this single command: you must love your neighbour as yourself. Love is the one thing that cannot hurt your neighbour: that is why it is the answer to every one of the commandments.

Romans 13:8–11

Help us to keep your commandments, so that through your Holy Spirit we may dwell in you, and you in us.

Bidding Prayer

Shed your clear light on our hearts, Lord,
that walking continually in the way of your
    commandments,
we may never be deceived or misled.

Morning Prayer

This is the covenant I will make with you – it is the Lord
who speaks. Deep within you I will plant my Law,
writing it on your hearts. Then I will be your God and
you shall be my people.

from *Jeremiah 31:33*

Love and do what you will.

St Augustine

When you have done all you have been told to do, say, 'We
are merely servants: we have done no more than our duty.'

Luke 17:10

UNITY

In the meantime brothers we wish you happiness; try to
be perfect; help one another. Be united; live in peace,
and the God of love and peace will be with you. The
grace of our Lord Jesus Christ, the love of God and the
fellowship of the Holy Spirit be with you all.

2 Corinthians 13:11–13

May the peace of Christ reign in your hearts, because it is
for this that you are called together as parts of one body.

Colossians 3:15

May he who helps us when we refuse to give up, help you
all to be tolerant with each other, following the example

of Christ Jesus, so that united in mind and voice you may give glory to the God and Father of our Lord Jesus Christ.

Romans 15:5–6

I implore you therefore to lead a life worthy of your vocation. Bear with one another charitably, in complete selflessness, gentleness and patience. Do all you can to preserve the unity of the Spirit by the peace that binds you together. There is one Body, one Spirit, just as you were all called into one and the same hope when you were called. There is one Lord, one faith, one baptism, and one God who is Father of all, over all, through all, and within all.

Ephesians 4:1–6

Each one of us, however, has been given his own share of grace, given as Christ allotted it. And to some, his gift was that they should be apostles; to some, prophets; to some, evangelists; to some, pastors and teachers; so that the saints together make a unity in the work of service, building up the Body of Christ. In this way we are all to come to unity in our faith and our knowledge of the Son of God, until we become perfect Man, fully mature with the fulness of Christ himself.

Ephesians 4:9–13

Let us pray that everyone
of every race and nation,
may acknowledge the one God as Father,
and in the bond of common brotherhood
seek his kingdom,
which is peace and joy in the Holy Spirit.

Bidding Prayer, Confirmation

✣

JESUS CHRIST, THE LIFE

God created man in the image of himself,
in the image of God he created them,
male and female he created them.

Genesis 1:27

Jesus said:
    'I have come so that they may have life,
    and have it to the full.'

John 10:10

Jesus died so that we could share God's life. To find this
fulness of life we must die to self, be converted, be patient
in our sufferings and uncertainties, be willing to grow in
hope and love. As we become more aware of God's presence in our lives, and of the world he has made, so we are
ready to adore, to praise and to thank him. By sharing the
life of Christ in his Church we discover something of the
freedom of the sons and daughters of God.

DEATH

Remember our brothers and sisters
who have gone to their rest

in the hope of rising again;
bring them and all the departed
into the light of your presence.

Eucharistic Prayer

Death was never of God's fashioning; not for his pleasure
does life cease to be; what meant his creation, but that
all created things should have being? No breed has he
created on earth but for its thriving; none carries in itself
the seeds of its own destruction. Think not that mortal-
ity bears sway on earth; no end or term is fixed to a life
well lived.

Wisdom 1:13–15

My soul is thirsting for God,
the God of my life;
when can I enter and see
the face of God?

Psalm 41(42):3

We pray for those who have died, and are on their way to
you, Lord.
Give them fulness of life and happiness.

We pray for those who are dying, Lord, and who are
afraid.
Give them strength to go on their last journey in peace.

We pray, Lord, for those who have been wounded by the
death of one they love.
Help them find the new life that comes through death.

We pray for those who are worried and anxious about
many things.
Help them, Lord, find peace in dying to themselves.

We pray for those who are depressed and in despair.
Show them, Lord, that by dying to self there is a birth
of hope.

Bidding Prayers

Lord, Lord, do you hear me?
Lord, show me my door,
take me by the hand.
Open the door,
show me the way,
the path leading to joy, to light.

Michel Quoist

Christ is the morning star
who when the darkness of this world is past
brings to his saints the promise of the light of life
and opens everlasting day.

St Bede

Let the absolving words be said over me, and the holy oil sign
and seal me, and thy own body be my food and thy blood my
sprinkling. And let my mother Mary breathe on me and my
angel whisper peace to me, and my saints smile on me ... that
in them all and through them all I may receive the gift of perseverance, and die, as I desire to live, in thy faith, in thy
Church, in thy service, and in thy love.

Cardinal Newman

Lord God,
you have prepared for those who love you
what no eye has seen, no ear has heard.
Fill our hearts with your love,
so that loving you above all and in all,
we may attain your promises
which the heart of man has not conceived.

Sunday Prayer

If we have died with him, then we shall live with him.
If we hold firm, then we shall reign with him.
If we disown him, then he will disown us.
We may be unfaithful, but he is always faithful,
for he cannot disown his own self.

2 Timothy 2:11–13

Day is done, but love unfailing
dwells ever here;
shadows fall, but hope prevailing
calms every fear.
Loving Father, none forsaking,
take our hearts, of love's own making,
watch our sleeping, guard our waking,
be always near!

Dark descends, but light unending
shines through our night;
you are with us, ever lending
new strength to sight;
one in love, your truth confessing,
one in hope of heaven's blessing,
may we see, in love's possessing,
love's endless light!

James Quinn

The throne of God and of the Lamb will be in its place in the city; his servants will worship him, they will see him face to face, and his name will be written on their foreheads. It will never be night again and they will not need lamplight or sunlight, because the Lord God will be shining on them. They will reign for ever and ever.

Revelation 22:3–5

Father, into your hands I commit my spirit.

Luke 23:46

I am the resurrection.
If anyone believes in me, even though he dies, he will
    live,
and whoever lives and believes in me
will never die.

John 11:25–26

I tell you most solemnly,
unless a wheat grain falls on the ground and dies,
it remains only a single grain;
but if it dies,
it yields a rich harvest.
Anyone who loves his life loses it;
anyone who hates his life in this world
will keep it for the eternal life.

John 12:24–25

I tell you most solemnly,
whoever keeps my word
will never see death.

John 8:51

Anyone who finds his life will lose it; anyone who loses his life for my sake will find it.

Matthew 10:39

Come, Lord Jesus, come!

Revelation 22:20

CONVERSION

Repent and be converted, for the kingdom of God is at hand.

Matthew 3:8

Give me, good Lord, a full faith and a fervent charity, a love of you, good Lord, incomparable above the love of myself; and that I love nothing to your displeasure but everything in an order to you.

Take from me, good Lord, this lukewarm fashion, or rather key-cold manner of meditation and this dullness in praying to you. And give me warmth, delight and life in thinking about you. And give me your grace to long for your holy Sacraments and specially to rejoice in the presence of your blessed Body, sweet Saviour Christ, in the holy Sacrament of the Altar, and duly to thank you for your gracious coming.

St Thomas More

The Son of Man has come to seek out and save what was lost.

Luke 19:10

As by your will you first strayed away from God, so now turn back and search for him ten times as hard.

Baruch 4:28–29

Soul of Christ, sanctify me.
Body of Christ, save me.
Water from the side of Christ, wash me.
Passion of Christ, strengthen me.
O Good Jesu, hear me.
Let me not be separated from you.
From the malicious enemy defend me.
In the hour of my death call me.
And bid me come to you,
so that with your saints I may praise you,
for ever and ever.   Amen.

The Anima Christi

I will make an everlasting covenant with them; I will not cease in my efforts for their good, and I will put respect for me into their hearts, so that they turn from me no more.

Jeremiah 32:40

I tell you solemnly, unless you change and become as little children, you will never enter the kingdom of heaven.

Matthew 18:3

Your mind must be renewed by a spiritual revolution, so that you can put on the new self that has been created in God's way, in the goodness and holiness of the truth.

Ephesians 4:24

O God, give me the sincerity
to accept the things I cannot change,
the courage to change the things I can,
and the wisdom to know the difference.

Rheinhold Niebuhr

PATIENCE

Suffering brings patience, as we know, and patience brings
perseverance, and perseverance brings hope, and this hope
is not deceptive, because the love of God has been poured
into our hearts by the Holy Spirit which has been given us.

Romans 5:4–5

With the Lord 'a day' can mean a thousand years. The
Lord is not being slow to carry out his promises, as anybody else might be called slow, but he is being patient
with you all, wanting nobody to be lost and everybody to
be brought to change his ways.

2 Peter 3:8–9

Love is always patient and kind.

1 Corinthians 13:4

Remember, O most loving Virgin Mary, that it is a thing
unheard of, that anyone ever had recourse to your protection,
implored your help, or sought your intercession, and was left
forsaken. Filled therefore with confidence in your goodness I fly
to you, O Mother, Virgin of virgins. To you I come, before you
I stand, a sorrowful sinner. Despise not my poor words, O Mother of the Word of God, but graciously hear and grant my prayer.

St Bernard

Lord, give me patience in tribulation. Let the memory of your Passion, and of those bitter pains you suffered for me, strengthen my patience and support me in this tribulation and adversity.

St John Forrest

Give patient tolerance, Lord, to all who are no longer young. Open the hearts of the young to accept from them understanding and love.

Bidding Prayer

Never disappoint the trust
another puts in you.
Be warm and merciful
and let none go from you empty-handed.
The least you can offer
is your time and patience,
your affection and your prayer.

Rule for a New Brother

O Lord my God, as you led your people through the desert, so lead me now through the desert of my failures to your kingdom. Light my way; show me your will; give me your Spirit of truth, so that I may know, love and serve you more faithfully.

SUFFERING

All shall be well, and all shall be well, and all manner of things shall be well.

Julian of Norwich

Lord, in answer to our prayer
give us patience in suffering hardships
after the example of your Only-begotten Son,
who lives and reigns for ever and ever.   Amen.

Midday Prayer

Lord, teach us to see you present in all people. Help us to recognise you most of all in those who suffer.

Bidding Prayer

My Father, if it is possible, let this cup pass me by. Nevertheless, let it be as you, not I, would have it. My Father, if this cup cannot pass by without my drinking it, your will be done!

Matthew 26:39, 42

The spirit is willing, but the flesh is weak.

Matthew 26:41

I think that what we suffer in this life can never be compared to the glory, as yet unrevealed, which is waiting for us. The whole creation is eagerly waiting for God to reveal his sons ... And not only creation, but all of us who possess the first fruits of the Spirit, we too groan inwardly as we wait for our bodies to be set free ... We must wait with patience.

from *Romans 8:18–25*

I have been crucified with Christ, and I live now not with my own life but with the life of Christ who lives in me.

Galatians 2:19–20

My God, my God, why have you forsaken me?
Do not leave me alone in my distress;
Come close, there is none else to help.

O Lord, do not leave me alone,
my strength, make haste to help me!

Psalm 21(22):2, 12, 20

Lord, be with those who are persecuted for their faith, and those cut off from the support of the Church; good Shepherd, in their pain and desolation may they know your tender care.

Bidding Prayer

GROWTH

What we ask God is that through perfect wisdom and spiritual understanding you should reach the fullest knowledge of his will. So you will be able to lead the kind of life the Lord expects of you, a life acceptable to him in all its aspects; showing the results in all the good actions you do and increasing your knowledge of God. You will have in you the strength, based on his own glorious power, never to give in, but to bear anything joyfully, thanking the Father who has made it possible for you to join the saints and with them to inherit the light.

Colossians 1:9–12

Do not let your love be a pretence, but sincerely prefer good to evil. Love each other as much as brothers should, and have a profound respect for each other. Work for the Lord with untiring effort and with great earnestness of spirit. If you have hope, this will make you cheerful. Do not give up if trials come; and keep on praying.

Romans 12:9–12

You will always have your trials but, when they come, try to treat them as a happy privilege; you understand that your faith is only put to the test to make you patient, but patience too is to have its practical result so that you will become fully developed, complete, with nothing missing.

James 1:2–4

The glory of God is man made fully alive.

St Irenaeus

How high thou art in the height, how deep in the depth. Thou never leavest us, yet how hard it is to return to thee. Come, Lord, and work. Arouse and incite us. Kindle us and sweep us onward. Be fragrant as flowers, sweet as honey. Teach us to love and to run.

St Augustine

Jesus said:
  'I tell you most solemnly
  if you do not eat the flesh of the Son of Man
  and drink his blood
  you will not have life in you.
  Anyone who does eat my flesh and drink my blood
  has eternal life,
  and I shall raise him up on the last day.

For my flesh is real food
and my blood is real drink.
He who eats my flesh and drinks my blood
lives in me
and I live in him ...
Anyone who eats this bread will live for ever.'

John 6:53–58

Almighty God and Father, you so loved the world that
you sent your Son to show us how to love without limit.
Teach me to accept your Spirit of love and truth so that
I may learn to live as your friend.

Personal growth is not optional for us ... God's will that
we must grow sums up our human duty.

Pope Paul VI

HOPE

The Lord is my shepherd;
there is nothing I shall want.
Fresh and green are the pastures
where he gives me repose.
Near restful waters he leads me,
to revive my drooping spirit.

Psalm 22(23):1–3

Let us be confident in approaching the throne of grace,
that we shall have mercy from him and find grace when
we are in need of help.

Hebrews 4:16

When I fear, I will trust in you
in God whose word I praise.
In God I trust, I shall not fear:
what can mortal man do to me?

Psalm 55(56):4–5

Jesus said: 'Today you will be with me in paradise.'

Luke 23:24

We are in difficulties on all sides, but never cornered; we see no answer to our problems, but never despair; we have been persecuted, but never deserted; knocked down, but never killed; always, wherever we may be we carry with us in our body the death of Jesus, so that the life of Jesus, too, may always be seen in our body.

2 Corinthians 4:8–10

O God, to whom all hearts are open, all desires known, and from whom no secrets are hidden, cleanse the thoughts of our hearts by the inpouring of your Holy Spirit, that every thought and word of ours may begin from you, and in you be perfectly completed, through Christ our Lord.   Amen.

A Confirmation Prayer

Redeem me Lord, and show me your mercy.

Psalm 25(26):11

A blessing on the man who puts his trust in the Lord,
with the Lord for his hope.
He is like a tree by the waterside,
that thrusts its roots to the stream:

when the heat comes it feels no alarm,
its foliage stays green;
it has no worries in a year of drought,
and never ceases to bear fruit.

Jeremiah 17:7–8

Lord, happy the man who trusts in you!

Psalm 33(34):9

O God, the creator and redeemer of all the faithful, grant
to the souls of your servants departed the remission of all
their sins, that through our prayers they may obtain that
pardon which they have always desired.

LOVE

Lord God,
you love us as a father loves his children.
Help us to respond to your gift
and learn to love without limit,
as did your Son,
Jesus Christ, our Lord.

Love is always patient and kind; it is never jealous; love
is never boastful or conceited; it is never rude or selfish;
it does not take offence, and is not resentful. Love takes
no pleasure in other people's sins but delights in
the truth; it is always ready to excuse, to trust, to hope,
and to endure whatever comes … There are three things
that last: faith, hope and love; and the greatest of these is
love.

1 Corinthians 13:4–13

God of your goodness give me yourself, for you are enough for me.

Julian of Norwich

May the Lord be generous in increasing your love and make you love one another and the whole human race ... and may he so confirm your hearts in holiness that you may be blameless in the sight of our God and Father when our Lord Jesus Christ comes with all his saints.

1 Thessalonians 3:12, 13

God is love
and anyone who lives in love lives in God,
and God lives in him.

1 John 4:16

The perfect lover longeth for to be
In presence of his love both night and day
And if it haply so befall that he may not be as he would,
He will yet as he may ever be with his love.

St Thomas More

Jesus, Jesus, Jesus
Jesus, Jesus, Jesus } Grant us grace to love you
Jesus, Jesus, Jesus

Jesus, grant us grace truly to love you for your great goodness and the generous gifts we have received, and hope always to receive from you.
Let the thought of your goodness and patience overcome our sinful inclinations.

Let the consideration of the times you have come into
our lives to help and save us, make us ashamed of our
ingratitude.

To think that you ask nothing of us in return, except that
we should love you, and you ask that only because you
are so good!

Dear Lord, our whole life shall be nothing but a desire for
you, and to show our love we shall keep your commandments faithfully.

Have mercy on all sinners, Jesus, we beg you; turn their
vices into virtues, convert their hearts to love of you
and your commandments and bring them to bliss in
everlasting glory.

Have mercy also on the souls in purgatory, for your bitter
Passion, we beg you, and for your glorious name, Jesus.
(Our Father ... Hail Mary ...)

from *The Jesus Psalter*

Let us love one another
since love comes from God
and everyone who loves is begotten by God and knows
God ...
No one has ever seen God;
but as long as we love one another
God will live in us
and his love will be complete in us ...
God is love
and anyone who lives in love
lives in God,
and God lives in him.

1 John 4:7–16

God loved the word so much
that he gave his only Son,
so that everyone who believes in him
may not be lost,
but may have eternal life.

John 3:16

Where true love is dwelling, God is dwelling there;
Love's own loving presence love does ever share.

Love of Christ has made us out of many one;
In our midst is dwelling God's eternal Son.

Give him joyful welcome, love him and revere;
Cherish one another with a love sincere.

James Quinn

O heart of love, I put all my trust in thee. For I fear all things
from my own weakness, but I hope for all things from thy
goodness.

St Margaret Mary

This is my commandment
love one another,
as I have loved you.

John 15:12

Our love is not to be just words and mere talk,
but something real and active.

1 John 3:18

For I am certain of this: neither death nor life, no angel,
no prince, nothing that exists, nothing still to come, not
any power, or height or depth, nor any created thing, can
ever come between us and the love of God made visible
in Christ Jesus our Lord.

Romans 8:35–39

Arise, Lord! Redeem us because of your love.

Psalm 43(44):27

Jesus, grant me the grace to love you.
O blessed Jesu, make me love you entirely.
O blessed Jesu, let me deeply consider your love for me.
O blessed Jesu, give me the grace to thank you for your
    gifts.
Sweet Jesu, possess my heart, hold and keep it for yourself
    alone.

St John Fisher

THE PRESENCE OF GOD

I will walk in the presence of the Lord
in the land of the living.

Psalm 114(115):9

Be still, and know that I am God.

Psalm 45(46):11

Where two or three meet in my name, I shall be there
with them.

Matthew 18:20

If anyone loves me he will keep my word,
and my Father will love him,
and we shall come to him
and make our home with him.

John 14:23

Alone with none but thee, my God,
   I journey on my way;
What need I fear, when thou art near,
   O King of night and day?
More safe am I within thy hand
Than if a host did round me stand.

St Columba

If anyone acknowledges that Jesus is the Son of God,
God lives in him and he in God.

1 John 4:15

We are enfolded in the Father, we are enfolded in the Son,
and we are enfolded in the Holy Spirit. And the Father is
enfolded in us, and the Son is enfolded in us, and the Holy
Spirit is enfolded in us.

Julian of Norwich

Lord, true light and creator of light,
grant that faithfully pondering on all that is holy,
we may ever live in the splendour of your presence.

Morning Prayer

O gracious and holy Father,
give us wisdom to perceive you,
intelligence to understand you,
diligence to seek you,
patience to wait for you,
eyes to behold you,
a heart to meditate upon you,
and a life to proclaim you;
through the power of the Spirit
of Jesus Christ our Lord.

St Benedict

God be in my head and in my understanding;
God be in mine eyes, and in my looking;
God be in my mouth, and in my speaking;
God be in my heart, and in my thinking;
God be at mine end, and at my departing.

Book of Hours, 1514

Glory be to him whose power, working in us, can do infinitely more than we can ask or imagine; glory be to him from generation to generation in the Church and in Christ Jesus for ever and ever.   Amen.

Ephesians 3:20–21

Through your faith, God's power will guard you until the salvation which has been prepared is revealed at the end of time.

1 Peter 1:5

O God come to my aid,
O Lord make haste to help me!

The Prayer of the Church

Christ was crucified through weakness, and still he lives now through the power of God. So then, we are weak, as he was, but we shall live with him, through the power of God.

2 Corinthians 13:4

My grace is enough for you: my power is at its best in weakness.

2 Corinthians 12:9

The Lord's right hand has triumphed;
his right hand raised me.
The Lord's right hand has triumphed;
I shall not die, I shall live.

Psalm 117(118):16–17

It were my soul's desire
to see the face of God;
it were my soul's desire
to rest in his abode.

Grant, Lord, my soul's desire,
deep waves of cleansing sighs,
grant, Lord, my soul's desire,
from earthly cares to rise.

It were my soul's desire
to imitate my King,
it were my soul's desire
his endless praise to sing.

It were my soul's desire,
when heaven's gate is won,
to find my soul's desire
clear shining like the sun.

This still my soul's desire,
whatever life afford,
to gain my soul's desire,
and see thy face, O Lord.

The Prayer of the Church

CREATION

O Lord, how great are your works,
how wonderful are your designs.

Psalm 91(92):6

God saw all he had made, and indeed it was very good.

Genesis 1:31

Long ago you founded the earth, Lord,
and the heavens are the work of your hands.

Psalm 101(102):26

Blessed are you, Lord, God of all creation.
Through your goodness we have ourselves to offer,
whom you have made and called to be your children.
May we live indeed as the work of your hands.
Blessed be God for ever.

An Offertory Prayer

The heavens proclaim the glory of God
and the firmament shows forth the work of his hands.
Day unto day takes up the story
and night unto night makes known the message.

No speech, no word, no voice is heard
yet their span extends through all the earth,
their words to the utmost bounds of the world.

There he has placed a tent for the sun;
it comes forth like a bridegroom coming from his tent,
rejoices like a champion to run its course.

At the end of the sky is the rising of the sun;
to the furthest end of the sky is its course.
There is nothing concealed from its burning heat.

Psalm 18(19)

O thou, who art the true sun of the world, ever rising, and never going down; who by thy most wholesome appearing and sight dost nourish and gladden all things in heaven and earth; we beseech thee mercifully to shine into our hearts, that the night and darkness of sin, and the mists of error on every side, being driven away by the brightness of thy shining within our hearts, we may all our life walk without stumbling, as in the day time, and being pure and clean from the works of darkness, may abound in all good works which thou hadst prepared for us to walk in.   Amen.

Erasmus

It was the Lord God who formed the mountains,
created the wind,
reveals his mind to man
makes both dawn and dark,
walks on the top of the heights of the world.

Amos 4:13

PRAISE AND THANKSGIVING

My soul, give thanks to the Lord,
all my being, bless his holy name.
My soul, give thanks to the Lord,
and never forget all his blessings.

Psalm 102(103):1–2

O give thanks to the Lord for he is good;
for his love endures for ever.

Psalm 106(107):1

Let everything that lives and that breathes give praise to
the Lord.

Psalm 150:6

The Lord gave, the Lord has taken back. Blessed be the
name of the Lord.

Job 1:21

Thanks be to you, my Lord Jesus Christ,
for all the benefits which you have given me,
for all the pains and insults
which you have borne for me.
O most merciful Redeemer, Friend and Brother,

may I know you more clearly,
love you more dearly,
follow you more nearly,
day by day.

St Richard of Chichester

Let the message of Christ, in all its richness, find a home
with you. Teach each other, and advise each other, in all
wisdom. With gratitude in your hearts sing psalms and
hymns and inspired songs to God; and never say or do
anything except in the name of the Lord Jesus, giving
thanks to God the Father through him.

Colossians 3:16–17

Whatever you eat, whatever you drink, whatever you do
at all, do it for the glory of God.

1 Corinthians 10:31

The Lord's is the earth and its fulness.
Come let us adore him!

Antiphon

Give thanks to the Lord for he is good,
for his love endures for ever.

Psalm 117(118):1

You are our Lord and our God, you are worthy of glory
and honour and power, because you made all the uni-
verse and it was only by your will that everything was
made and exists.

Revelation 4:11

How rich are the depths of God – how deep his wisdom and knowledge – and how impossible to penetrate his motives or understand his methods! Who could ever know the mind of the Lord? Who could ever be his counsellor? Who could ever give him anything or lend him anything? All that exists comes from him; all is by him and for him. To him be glory for ever!   Amen.

Romans 11:33–36

THE CHURCH

Jesus put another parable before them: 'The kingdom of heaven is like a mustard seed which a man took and sowed in his field. It is the smallest of all the seeds, but when it has grown it is the biggest shrub of all and becomes a tree so that the birds of the air come and shelter in its branches.'

He told them another parable: 'The kingdom of heaven is like the yeast a woman took and mixed in with three measures of flour till it was leavened all through.' ...

And again: 'The kingdom of heaven is like treasure hidden in a field which someone has found: he hides it again, goes off happy, sells everything he owns and buys the field.

'Again, the kingdom of heaven is like a merchant looking for fine pearls; when he finds one of great value he goes and sells everything he owns and buys it.

'Again, the kingdom of heaven is like a dragnet cast into the sea that brings in a haul of all kinds. When it is full, the fishermen haul it ashore; then, sitting down, they collect the good ones in a basket and throw away those that are no use.'

Matthew 13:31–49

Jesus said, 'You are Peter and upon this rock I will build my Church. And the gates of the underworld can never hold out against it. I will give you the keys of the kingdom of heaven; whatever you bind on earth shall be considered bound in heaven; whatever you loose on earth shall be considered loosed in heaven.'

Matthew 16:18–19

They remained faithful to the teaching of the apostles, to the brotherhood, to the breaking of bread and to the prayers ...

The faithful all lived together and owned everything in common; they sold their goods and possessions and shared out the proceeds amongst themselves according to what each needed.

They went as a body to the temple every day but met in their houses for the breaking of the bread; they shared their food gladly and generously; they praised God and were looked up to by everyone. Day by day the Lord added to their community those destined to be saved.

Acts 2:42–47

You shall be my people. I will be your God.

Ezekiel 36:28

You are a chosen race, a royal priesthood, a consecrated nation, a people set apart to sing the praises of God who called you out of darkness into his wonderful light. Once you were not a people at all and now you are the People of God.

1 Peter 2:9–10

May your Church, Lord, be a light to the nations, the sign and source of your power to unite all people. May she lead mankind to the mystery of your love.

Bidding Prayer

FREEDOM

The Law, of course, as we all know, is spiritual; but I am unspiritual; I have been sold as a slave to sin. I cannot understand my own behaviour. I fail to carry out the things I want to do, and I find myself doing the very things I hate. When I act against my own will, that means I have a self that acknowledges that the Law is good, and so the thing behaving in that way is not my self but sin living in me. The fact is, I know of nothing good living in me – living, that is, in my unspiritual self – for though the will to do what is good is in me, the performance is not, with the result that instead of doing the good things I want to do, I carry out the sinful things I do not want. When I act against my will, then, it is not my true self doing it, but sin which lives in me. In fact, this seems to be the rule, that every single time I want to do good it is something evil that comes to hand. In my inmost self I dearly love God's Law, but I can see that my body dictates a different law that battles against the law which my reason dictates. This is what makes me a prisoner of that law of sin which lives inside my body. What a wretched man I am! Who will rescue me from this body doomed to death? Thanks be to God through Jesus Christ our Lord!

Romans 7:14–25

The man who looks steadily at the perfect law of freedom and makes that his habit – not listening and then forgetting, but actively putting it into practice – will be happy in all that he does.

James 1:25

You, Lord, are the source of our freedom. Bring those in captivity of mind or body to the freedom of the children of God.

Bidding Prayer

If the Son makes you free,
you will be free indeed.

John 8:36

A slave, when he is called in the Lord, becomes the Lord's freedman, and a freeman called in the Lord becomes Christ's slave.

1 Corinthians 7:22

If in union with Christ we have imitated his death, we shall also imitate him in his resurrection. We must realise that our former selves have been crucified with him to destroy this sinful body and to free us from the slavery of sin. When a man dies, of course, he has finished with sin.

Romans 6:5–7

If you make my word your own
you will indeed be my disciples,
you will learn the truth
and the truth will make you free.

John 8:31–32

All baptised in Christ, you have all clothed yourselves in Christ, and there are no more distinctions between Jew and Greek, slave and free, male and female, but all of you are one in Christ Jesus.

Galatians 3:27–28

You are slaves of no one except God, so behave like free men, and never use your freedom as an excuse for wickedness. Have respect for everyone and love for our community.

1 Peter 2:16–17

Everyone moved by the Spirit is a son of God. The spirit you received is not the spirit of slaves bringing fear into your lives again; it is the spirit of sons, and it makes us cry out, 'Abba, Father!' The Spirit himself and our spirit bear united witness that we are children of God. And if we are children we are heirs as well: heirs of God and coheirs with Christ, sharing his sufferings so as to share his glory.

Romans 8:14–17

The spirit of the Lord has been given to me,
for he has anointed me.
He has sent me to bring the good news to the poor,
to proclaim liberty to captives
and to the blind new sight,
to set the downtrodden free,
to proclaim the Lord's year of favour.

Isaiah 61:1–2

✛

NIGHT PRAYER

We end the day as we began it, by remembering God's presence.

In the name of the Father,
and of the Son,
and of the Holy Spirit.   Amen.

Save us, Lord, while we are awake;
protect us while we sleep;
that we may keep watch with Christ
and rest with him in peace.

God has been with us throughout the day, but there may have been moments when we forgot his love and turned from him. We may pray for forgiveness:

Turn your ear, O Lord, and give answer
for I am poor and needy.
Preserve my life, for I am faithful:
save the servant who trusts in you.

You are my God, have mercy on me, Lord,
for I cry to you all day long.

Give joy to your servant, O Lord,
for to you I lift up my soul.

O Lord, you are good and forgiving,
full of love to all who call.
Give heed, O Lord, to my prayer
and attend to the sound of my voice.

In the day of distress I will call
and surely you will reply.

Psalm 85(86):1–7

He will always reply, but he asks us to know ourselves so that
we may grow in holiness. Pause for a moment to see how you
have lived today.

A prayer of sorrow

Lord God, our loving Father,
you know all my sins and failures,
my weaknesses and temptations.
I come to you with deep sorrow in my heart
for the wrong I have done and for the good I have
    failed to do
Forgive me, accept me, and strengthen me,
now and always.   Amen.

A traditional prayer of sorrow

My God, I am sorry and ask forgiveness for my sins.
By the help of your grace I will try not to sin again.

There are many wonderful prayers of sorrow among the Psalms; see especially Psalm 50(51).

Despite any failures there may have been today, it will have been a day, like every day, marked by God's care and blessing. Remember quietly the good moments – the success, the happiness, the laughter, the peacefulness – and give thanks to God for them.

* Lord, I thank you for all you have done for me today.
  Help me to see you more clearly in my life.

* Remember, Lord, all those I love.
  Teach me to be more generous towards them.

* Stay close, Lord, to those who have been with me today.
  Comfort those whom I have harmed;
  forgive those who may have hurt me;
  bless those who have encouraged me.

* May the work I have done today, Lord,
  give glory to you
  and be of service to my neighbour.

A prayer of happiness and peace

Preserve me, God, I take refuge in you.
I say to the Lord: 'You are my God.
My happiness lies in you alone.'

O Lord, it is you who are my portion and cup;
it is you yourself who are my prize.
The lot marked out for me is my delight:
welcome indeed the heritage that falls to me!

I will bless the Lord who gives me counsel,
who even at night directs my heart.
I keep the Lord ever in my sight;
since he is at my right hand, I shall stand firm.

And so my heart rejoices, my soul is glad;
even my body shall rest in safety.
You will show me the path of life,
the fulness of joy in your presence,
at your right hand happiness for ever.

from *Psalm 15(16)*

There is a time to pray for the peace that comes at the end of
life:
May the Lord support us all the day long,
till the shades lengthen and the evening comes,
and the busy world is hushed,
and the fever of life is over,
and our work is done.
Then in his mercy
may he give us a safe lodging,
and a holy rest,
and peace at the last.　　Amen.

Cardinal Newman

As we end the day we can remember again that we belong to the whole family of the saints, and ask Mary, our mother, to pray for us:

Hail, Holy Queen, Mother of Mercy!
Hail our life, our sweetness and our hope.
To you do we cry, poor banished children of Eve;
to you do we send up our sighs,
mourning and weeping in this vale of tears.
Turn, then, most gracious advocate,
your eyes of mercy towards us;
and after this our exile,
show unto us the blessed fruit of your womb, Jesus.
O clement, O loving, O sweet Virgin Mary.

May the Lord grant me a quiet night, and a perfect end.
Amen.